I0410375

July 2014

ENVIRONMENTAL REGULATION

EPA Should Improve Adherence to Guidance for Selected Elements of Regulatory Impact Analyses

GAO-14-519

ENVIRONMENTAL REGULATION

EPA Should Improve Adherence to Guidance for Selected Elements of Regulatory Impact Analyses

GAO Highlights

Highlights of GAO-14-519, a report to congressional requesters

Why GAO Did This Study

Federal regulations, especially those addressing health, safety, and the environment, can generate hundreds of billions of dollars in benefits and costs to society annually. Various statutes, executive orders, and OMB guidance direct federal agencies to analyze the benefits and costs of proposed regulations. These analyses—known as RIAs—can also provide affected entities, agencies, Congress, and the public with important information about the potential effects of new regulations.

According to OMB, EPA regulations account for the majority of the estimated benefits and costs of major federal regulations. GAO was asked to review EPA's RIAs for recent regulations. This report examines how EPA has used RIAs during the rulemaking process and the extent to which EPA adhered to OMB guidance on selected elements of RIAs for recent rules. GAO reviewed RIAs from a nonprobability sample of seven recent air, water, and other environmental regulations, assessed them against relevant OMB guidance, and interviewed agency officials.

What GAO Recommends

GAO recommends that EPA improve adherence to OMB guidance and enhance the usefulness of its RIAs, and that OMB clarify the application of guidance for estimating the benefits of reducing greenhouse gas emissions. In commenting on a draft of this report, EPA stated that it generally agreed with GAO's recommendations. On behalf of OMB, in oral comments OMB staff said that they neither agreed nor disagreed with the recommendations but saw some merit in them.

View GAO-14-519. For more information, contact J. Alfredo Gomez at (202) 512-3841 or gomezj@gao.gov.

What GAO Found

The Environmental Protection Agency (EPA) used the seven Regulatory Impact Analyses (RIA) GAO reviewed to inform decision making, and its adherence to relevant Office of Management and Budget (OMB) guidance varied. According to senior EPA officials, the agency used these RIAs to facilitate communication with management throughout the rulemaking process and communicate information that supported its regulatory decisions to Congress and the public. However, it generally did not use them as the primary basis for final regulatory decisions.

EPA generally adhered to many aspects of OMB's Circular A-4 guidance for analyzing the economic effects of regulations including, for example, considering regulatory alternatives and analyzing uncertainties underlying its RIAs. However, EPA did not always adhere to other aspects. Specifically, the information EPA included and presented in the RIAs was not always clear. According to OMB guidance, RIAs should communicate information supporting regulatory decisions and enable a third party to understand how the agency arrives at its conclusions. In addition, EPA's review process does not ensure that the information about selected elements that should appear in the analyses—such as descriptions of baselines and alternatives considered—is transparent or clear, within and across its RIAs. As a result, EPA cannot ensure that its RIAs adhere to OMB's guidance to provide the public with a clear understanding of its decision making.

In addition to using Circular A-4 (issued in 2003) to analyze the effects of regulations, EPA used more recent guidance developed by an interagency working group co-led by OMB and another White House office in 2010 for valuing carbon dioxide emissions. Applying this guidance while using Circular A-4 to estimate other benefits and costs yielded inconsistencies in some of EPA's estimates and has raised questions about whether its approach was consistent with Circular A-4. Circular A-4 does not reference the new guidance and the new guidance does not include an overall statement explaining its relationship to Circular A-4. Without increased clarity about the relationship, questions about the agencies' adherence to OMB guidance will likely persist.

In assessing EPA's adherence to OMB guidance, GAO identified two other areas in which EPA faced challenges that limited the usefulness of some of its estimates. First, EPA did not monetize certain benefits and costs related to the primary purposes or key impacts of the rules GAO reviewed, such as reducing hazardous air pollutants and water quality effects. EPA officials said resource and data limitations constrained the agency's ability to monetize these effects. OMB guidance acknowledges that monetizing effects is not always possible. However, without doing so, the public may face challenges understanding the trade-offs associated with regulatory alternatives. Second, EPA estimated effects of its regulations on employment, in part, using a study that, according to EPA officials, represented the best reasonably obtainable data when they conducted their analyses. However, the study was based on data that were more than 20 years old and may not have represented the regulated entities addressed in the RIAs. EPA officials said they are exploring new approaches for analyzing these effects but were uncertain about when such results would be available. Without improvements in its estimates, EPA's RIAs may be limited in their usefulness for helping decision makers and the public understand these important effects.

Contents

Abbreviations

ADP	Action Development Process
CISWI	commercial and industrial solid waste incineration unit
EISA	Energy Independence and Security Act of 2007
ELG	effluent limitations guidelines
EPA	Environmental Protection Agency
EPAct	Energy Policy Act
OIRA	Office of Information and Regulatory Affairs
OMB	Office of Management and Budget
MACT	maximum achievable control technology
NHTSA	National Highway Traffic Safety Administration
RIA	Regulatory Impact Analysis

July 18, 2014

The Honorable Darrell Issa
Chairman
Committee on Oversight and Government Reform
House of Representatives

The Honorable David Vitter
Ranking Member
Committee on Environment and Public Works
United States Senate

Federal regulations, especially those addressing health, safety, and the environment, can generate substantial benefits and costs to society. For example, regulations aimed at decreasing the health risks associated with air pollution may require regulated entities such as power plants to install pollution control technologies. According to the Office of Management and Budget (OMB), from fiscal years 2001 through 2011, the Environmental Protection Agency's (EPA) regulations account for the majority of the estimated benefits and costs of major federal regulations. EPA issues regulations under environmental statutes to protect public health, improve air and water quality, and govern hazardous waste management, among other things. In 2012, OMB reported estimated annual benefits from major federal regulations totaling $141 billion to $691 billion and estimated annual costs of $42.4 billion to $66.3 billion for fiscal years 2001 through 2011, with EPA regulations accounting for 60 to 82 percent of the benefits and 43 to 53 percent of the costs.[1]

Recognizing the far reaching effects of regulations on individuals, firms, industries, and government agencies, various statutes, executive orders, and OMB guidance direct federal agencies to prepare and use economic analysis in regulatory decision making. Agencies can use economic analysis of regulatory alternatives—known as Regulatory Impact Analysis (RIA)—to help assess whether the benefits of an action justify the costs

---

[1]OMB, *2012 Report to Congress on the Benefits and Costs of Federal Regulations and Unfunded Mandates on State, Local, and Tribal Entities* (Washington, D.C., 2012). OMB included in these estimates (reported in 2001 dollars) only the regulations they reviewed for which agencies quantified and monetized a substantial portion of both benefits and costs.

and identify a regulatory alternative that yields the greatest net benefits (benefits minus costs). In addition, RIAs can provide affected entities, government agencies, Congress, and the public with important information about the potential effects of new regulations. An RIA is one component of the decision-making process. Other factors that may influence decision makers' selection of regulatory options include enforceability, technical feasibility, affordability, statutory or legal mandates, and ethical concerns.

Executive Order 12866 generally directs federal agencies, including EPA, to assess the economic effects of their economically significant rules—those with an annual effect on the economy of $100 million or more or that have a material adverse effect on a sector of the economy; productivity; competition; jobs; the environment; public health or safety; or state, local, or tribal governments or communities—and prepare a detailed RIA.[2] EPA carries out its regulatory responsibilities under a complex set of environmental laws, such as the Clean Air Act and the Clean Water Act. Its various program offices—including the Office of Air and Radiation, the Office of Chemical Safety and Pollution Prevention, the Office of Solid Waste and Emergency Response, and the Office of Water—implement these environmental laws by developing regulations and preparing associated RIAs, when relevant.

In 2003, OMB issued Circular A-4 to provide guidance to federal agencies for conducting regulatory analysis as directed by Executive Order 12866.[3] The guidance defines good regulatory analysis and provides best practices for conducting regulatory analysis. In particular, the guidance provides for systematic evaluation of qualitative and quantitative benefits and costs, including their monetization.[4] According to Circular A-4, a good RIA should include: (1) a statement of the need for the proposed action and an executive summary, (2) an examination of alternative approaches, (3) an evaluation of the benefits and costs—quantitative and qualitative—

---

[2]Executive Order, 12866, 58 Fed. Reg. 51735 (1993). Economically significant rules are a subset of significant rules as defined in Executive Order 12866. For these rules, Executive Order 12866 places greater emphasis on analyzing and quantifying the benefits and costs of the regulatory action.

[3]OMB, *Circular A-4: Regulatory Analysis* (Washington, D.C.: Sept. 17, 2003). Circular A-4 replaces OMB's "best practices" guidance issued in 1996 and 2000.

[4]Monetization is the process of estimating the dollar value of benefits and costs.

of the proposed action and the main alternatives identified by the analysis, and (4) a description of assumptions and treatment of uncertainty. It also acknowledges that agencies cannot analyze all regulations according to a formula, and that different regulations may call for different emphasis in the analysis. Executive Order 12866 and OMB Circular A-4 also specify that agencies should clearly articulate the basis for their estimates and conclusions. Executive Order 12866 specifies that agencies should provide information to the public in plain, understandable language, and OMB Circular A-4 guidance specifies that the elements of the analysis and development of estimates should be understandable to a qualified third-party reader.

EPA has also developed its own guidance for conducting economic analyses that emphasizes and reaffirms the principles in the Executive Order and OMB Circular A-4.[5] This guidance seeks to ensure that EPA's economic analyses inform the policy-making process and satisfy OMB's requirements for regulatory review by, among other things, developing a framework for economic analyses across EPA program offices and ensuring that the agency treats important subjects such as uncertainty, timing, and valuation of costs and benefits, consistently in all economic analyses.

You asked us to review selected elements of economic analyses EPA has used to support recent rulemakings. This report examines how EPA has used economic analyses in its decision making during the rulemaking process and the extent to which EPA adhered to OMB guidance in conducting selected elements of the economic analyses the agency used to support recent rulemakings.

To respond to this objective, we reviewed the RIAs from a nonprobability sample of seven recent rules and assessed them against key principles outlined in OMB Circular A-4 (see table 1 below for a list of the rules). We selected a nonprobability sample of rules that were: (1) economically significant under Executive Order 12866; (2) finalized in 2009 through 2011; (3) conducted by four different EPA program offices (Air and Radiation, Chemical Safety and Pollution Prevention, Solid Waste and Emergency Response, and Water); and (4) expected to have a varying

---

[5]EPA, *Guidelines for Preparing Economic Analyses*, 240-R-00-003 (Washington, D.C.: September 2000, updated December 2010, 240-R-10-001).

range of effects on the economy. Because this was a nonprobability sample, findings from our review of the seven rules cannot be generalized to those we did not review.

Table 1: Nonprobability Sample of Seven Economically Significant Rules EPA Finalized from 2009 through 2011

Rule title	Short title	Date final rule published
Office of Air and Radiation		
Greenhouse Gas Emissions Standards and Fuel Efficiency Standards for Medium- and Heavy-Duty Engines and Vehicles	Medium- and Heavy-Duty GHG	September 15, 2011
National Emissions Standards for Hazardous Air Pollutants for Major Sources: Industrial, Commercial, and Institutional Boilers and Process Heaters	Boiler MACT	March 21, 2011
Regulation of Fuels and Fuel Additives: Changes to Renewable Fuel Standard Program	RFS2	March 26, 2010
Standards of Performance for New Stationary Sources and Emission Guidelines for Existing Sources: Commercial and Industrial Solid Waste Incineration Units	CISWI	March 21, 2011
Office of Chemical Safety and Pollution Prevention		
Lead; Amendment to the Opt-out and Recordkeeping Provisions in the Renovation, Repair, and Painting Program	Lead Opt-Out	May 6, 2010
Office of Solid Waste and Emergency Response		
Oil Pollution Prevention; Spill Prevention, Control, and Countermeasure Rule—Amendments	SPCC	November 13, 2009
Office of Water		
Effluent Limitations Guidelines and Standards for the Construction and Development Point Source Category	ELG	December 1, 2009

Source: GAO. | GAO-14-519

Note: We limited our review to the versions of these rules finalized on the dates listed. We did not review changes, amendments, or other regulatory activity that occurred subsequent to the final issuance dates for the rules listed above.

We interviewed EPA officials responsible for preparing the RIAs to determine how EPA used them in its regulatory decision-making process and to clarify our review of the selected elements. The selected elements we assessed included the RIAs' statement of need and the inclusion and usefulness of an executive summary; treatment of regulatory alternatives; estimation of benefits and costs; and treatment of uncertainty, assumptions, and descriptions of data quality.[6] To assess the extent to which EPA adhered to OMB's guidance in Circular A-4 for selected elements of the RIAs, we developed a checklist that included questions related to each element. For each RIA, two analysts (including one economist) independently reviewed the analyses and subsequently came to consensus about each element's adherence to OMB guidance. In addition, we considered whether EPA clearly explained its analytical methods. We also spoke with selected economists with expertise in certain subject areas. Appendix I provides a more detailed description of our objectives, scope, and methodology, and appendix II provides descriptions of the rules we reviewed.

We conducted this performance audit from February 2012 to July 2014 in accordance with generally accepted government auditing standards. Those standards require that we plan and perform the audit to obtain sufficient, appropriate evidence to provide a reasonable basis for our findings and conclusions based on our audit objectives. We believe that the evidence obtained provides a reasonable basis for our findings and conclusions based on our audit objectives.

Background

Regulation is one of the principal tools the federal government uses to implement public policy. Agencies' rulemaking processes generally share three basic phases: (1) initiation of rulemaking actions, (2) development of proposed rules, and (3) issuance of final rules. Agencies' rulemaking processes include opportunities for internal and external deliberations and reviews, and, as appropriate, procedures for the development of an RIA. Figure 1 provides an overview of these rulemaking phases, including how agencies incorporate RIAs into the overall rulemaking process, when applicable.

---

[6]According to OMB guidance, agencies should analyze and present the important uncertainties connected with regulatory decisions as part of the overall regulatory analysis. Specifically, agencies should consider both the statistical variability of key elements underlying the estimates of benefits and costs and the incomplete knowledge about the relevant relationship.

Figure 1: Basic Phases of Rulemaking and Regulatory Impact Analysis Development Processes

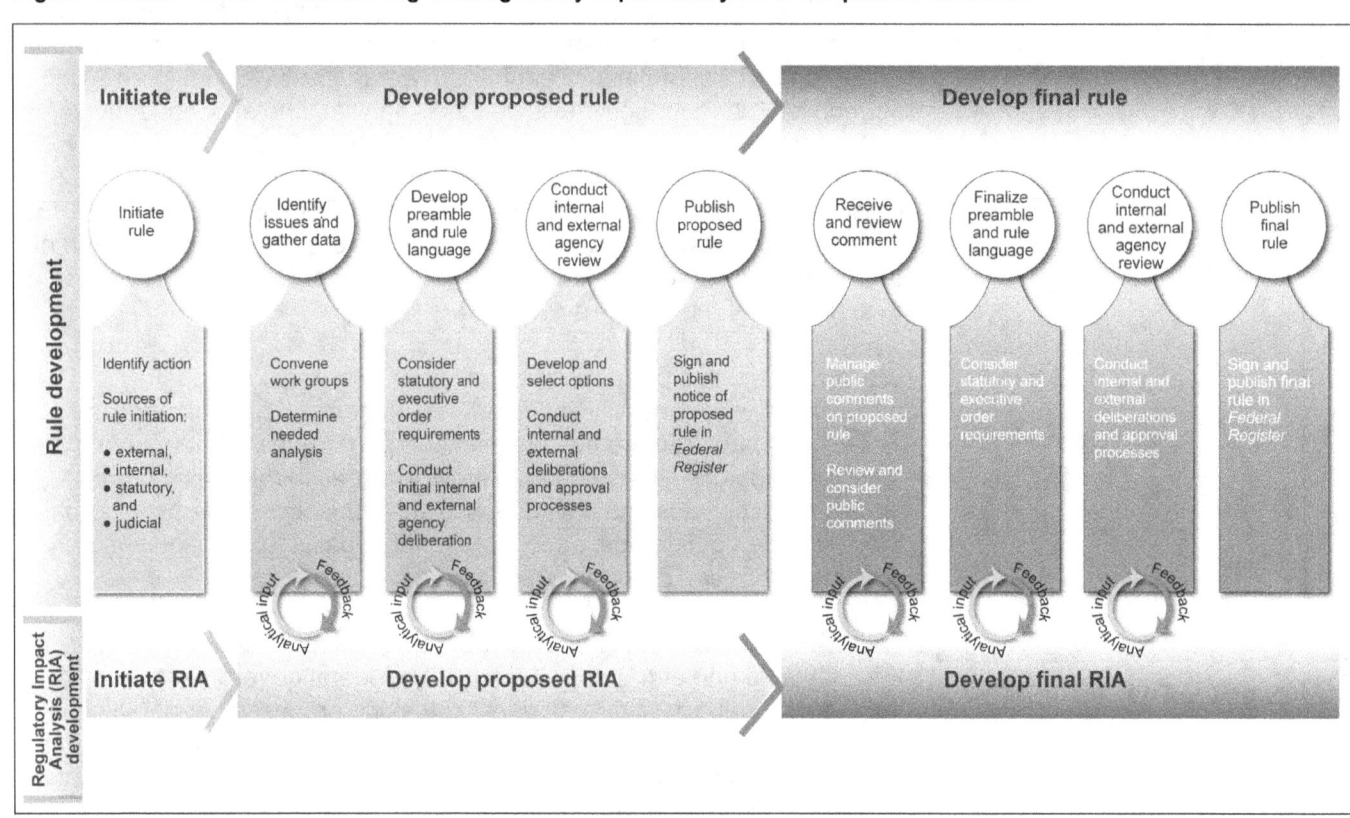

Source: GAO analysis of EPA data. | GAO-14-519

Note: The Regulatory Impact Analysis (RIA) development process provides analytical input into the rulemaking process and is informed by feedback from the rule development process.

During initiation, agency officials identify issues that may result in a rulemaking, including those resulting from statutory requirements or management agendas, for example. During this phase, agencies gather information that allows them to determine the need for a rulemaking. The second phase of the rulemaking process starts when an agency begins developing the proposed rule. During this phase, an agency will draft the rule and begin to address the analytical and procedural requirements, including commencing work on the RIA, when applicable. Rule development generally includes input from a wide range of disciplines, including engineers, scientists, economists, lawyers, and policy and subject matter experts, among others. For each rule the agency or the Administrator of the Office of Information and Regulatory Affairs (OIRA) within OMB identifies as an economically significant regulatory action, the agency develops the proposed rule and associated RIA and submits them to OIRA for formal review. After OIRA completes its review, and the agency incorporates resulting changes, the agency publishes the proposed rule in the Federal Register for public comment. In the third phase, development of the final rule, the agency responds to public comments, in some cases modifying the proposed rule in response to the comments. This phase also includes further internal and external review. The agency submits the final RIA and rule to OIRA for review before it publishes the final rule.

While agencies' rulemaking processes generally share these basic process steps, the agencies may vary in managing them. EPA uses the Action Development Process (ADP)—a series of steps the agency follows when it develops actions such as regulations and policy statements—to ensure that the agency adequately addresses scientific, economic, and policy issues at appropriate stages. In addition, the ADP provides opportunities for senior management to provide guidance and direction to staff and helps ensure input from across EPA offices. For economically significant rules, ADP steps generally include forming a workgroup of representatives from various EPA offices who will develop the action; preparing and executing an analytic blueprint for analyses needed to support the action; receiving early guidance from management; developing and selecting options that best achieve the goal of the action; drafting the proposed rule; and conducting final agency review.[7] The lead program office uses the ADP to direct the workgroup and their managers who provided policy direction and to help ensure the integrity of the process. In addition, EPA's National Center for Environmental Economics provides guidance for performing economic analysis and performs a regulatory review function for the agency by reviewing economic analysis underlying significant regulatory actions. It also conducts research and development on methods for analyzing economic effects.

Overall, OMB guidance states RIAs should measure the benefits and costs of a proposed action and the alternatives in comparable terms to

---

[7]An analytic blueprint spells out a workgroup's plans for the data collection and analyses that will support development of a specific action. It describes how the workgroup will collect, peer review, and use the information to craft the action within a specific budget and time frame. In addition, the analytic blueprint process potentially expands EPA's opportunities to consider a broad range of possible regulatory (and nonregulatory) strategies, including alternative or innovative approaches.

ensure a reasonable determination of net benefits. When estimating net benefits, the guidance states that agencies should generally estimate benefits and costs that accrue to society, including those that accrue only to private entities.[8] In addition, agencies should measure benefits and costs against a baseline that generally describes the expected state of the world without the regulation. The guidance also states that agencies should monetize benefits and costs whenever possible. Where agencies cannot monetize or quantify benefits and costs, guidance directs agencies to present the relevant qualitative information along with a description of the unquantified effects, and a discussion of the strengths and limitations of the qualitative information.

In considering alternatives, OMB guidance states that, by measuring incremental benefits and costs of regulatory alternatives, agencies can identify the alternative that maximizes net benefits, regardless of whether the agency selects that alternative. Because the benefits and costs of the regulatory action will occur in the future, agencies should adjust the value of future benefits and costs for differences in timing by applying an appropriate discount rate—the interest rate used to convert benefits and costs occurring in different time periods to a common present value. OMB guidance directs agencies to use 3 and 7 percent discount rates but allows agencies to apply other rates under special circumstances (e.g., when comparing benefits and costs across generations).[9] The guidance also states that agencies should explicitly identify the assumptions, methods, and data underlying their economic analyses, and the uncertainty associated with the resulting estimates. To help quantify the effect of uncertainty on benefit and cost estimates, agencies may use sensitivity or other types of analyses.[10] In addition, the guidance directs agencies to document that they based the analysis on the best

---

[8]Private costs are those paid by a consumer or firm. Social costs include both private costs plus any other external costs incurred by society resulting from the production or consumption of a good or service.

[9]According to OMB guidance, the 7 percent rate approximates the average before-tax rate of return on capital investments in the private sector, whereas the 3 percent rate approximates the rate at which consumers discount future consumption flows to their present value. Generally, using a higher discount rate gives less weight to future year benefits and gives more weight to near-term benefits.

[10]A sensitivity analysis assigns a variety of numerical values to key parameters, such as the compliance rate, to gauge the sensitivity of the benefit and cost estimates to these different values.

reasonably obtainable scientific, technical, and economic information. OMB guidance allows agencies to use professional judgment regarding the thoroughness of the analysis, while stressing the importance of full disclosure, including whether and how clearly the agencies explained their methods.

OMB last revised its guidance for regulatory analysis in 2003. Since that time, greater emphasis has been placed on agencies' ability to analyze certain effects—including the effects of regulations on employment and reductions in greenhouse gas emissions, such as carbon dioxide—that OMB's Circular A-4 does not specifically address. To ensure consistency across agencies in estimating benefits and costs related to reducing greenhouse gas emissions, in 2009, OMB co-convened an interagency working group to assess the best methods for valuing the benefits of reducing carbon dioxide emissions, known as the social cost of carbon.[11] The interagency working group produced a technical support document that summarized its work, including the assumptions and uncertainties that underlie the range of estimates it developed for quantifying the social cost of carbon.[12]

---

[11] The interagency working group defined social cost of carbon (measured in dollars per metric ton of carbon dioxide) as an estimate of the monetized damages associated with an incremental increase in carbon emissions in a given year. It is intended to include changes in net agricultural productivity, human health, property damages from increased flood risk, and the value of ecosystems due to climate change.

[12] Interagency Working Group on Social Cost of Carbon, United States Government, *Technical Support Document: Social Cost of Carbon for Regulatory Impact Analysis under Executive Order 12866* (Washington, D.C.: February 2010). In 2013, the interagency working group revised the 2010 estimates based on updated modeling results.

EPA Generally Used RIAs to Inform Decision Making and Varied In Adherence to OMB Guidance for Selected Elements of RIAs

EPA generally used the seven RIAs we reviewed to inform decision making during the rulemaking process but did not always adhere to OMB guidance for selected elements of these RIAs. According to EPA officials, the agency most commonly used these RIAs to facilitate an iterative process with management, identify effects of regulations, and communicate the information supporting EPA's regulatory decisions to Congress and the public. In addition, EPA's adherence to OMB guidance varied across selected elements of the RIAs we reviewed: (1) statements of need and inclusion and usefulness of an executive summary; (2) treatment of regulatory alternatives; (3) estimation of benefits and costs; and (4) treatment of uncertainty, assumptions, and descriptions of data quality.

EPA Used RIAs to Inform Decision Making

For the seven RIAs we reviewed, EPA officials said they used RIAs to inform decision making but did not use them as the primary basis for selecting the final regulatory option, with one exception. For example, for the Medium- and Heavy-Duty GHG rule, EPA officials said they used the RIA as the primary basis for identifying and selecting from the alternatives considered the most technically feasible option with the greatest net benefits. However, for another rule—RFS2—EPA officials said the RIA played no role in selecting a regulatory approach because the approach resulted from a congressional mandate included in the Energy Independence and Security Act of 2007. Instead, EPA used this RIA to identify the effects of the mandate for Congress and the public, according to EPA officials. For the other five rules, EPA officials said the RIAs facilitated an iterative process with management and communicated information to Congress and the public that supported the regulatory decision. For example, for SPCC, EPA economists said they used information gathered during the analysis to clarify misconceptions decision makers had about the proposed regulation. In addition, EPA used the CISWI and Boiler MACT RIAs to communicate the effects of two standards to which their authorizing law—the Clean Air Act—refers.

EPA Generally Adhered to Guidance to Include Statements of Need and Executive Summaries, but Overall, Information in the RIAs Was Not Always Clear or Complete

All seven of the RIAs we reviewed generally adhered to OMB guidance calling for statements of need for the proposed regulatory actions, but these statements were not always clear. OMB guidance states that an agency must demonstrate the need for the proposed action before recommending regulatory action and only promulgate those required by law, necessary to interpret the law, or made necessary by a compelling need, such as material failures of private markets to protect or improve the health and safety of the public or the environment. Accordingly, the guidance states that the RIA should include a statement of need that identifies and explains the problem that the proposed regulation seeks to address—for example, a market failure, or some other compelling public need.[13]

In several of the RIAs we reviewed, EPA clearly explained the problem the regulation intended to address and did so early in the analysis. For example, in the ELG RIA, EPA clearly identified and explained the market failure the regulation was intended to address and the authority under which it was promulgated. However, in other RIAs, EPA provided a less explicit explanation. For example, the CISWI RIA included information about the need for the rule, but it did not explicitly describe the problem the rule sought to address. Similarly, in the RFS2 RIA, EPA explained the need for the proposed rule—to assess the projected impacts of the renewable fuel volumes established through the Energy Independence and Security Act of 2007—but did not describe the problem the rule intended to address. According to EPA officials, in both of these cases, the preamble of the final rule published in the Federal Register included this information. Nonetheless, without a clear description of the problem the regulation is intended to address in the RIA, the context and rationale for the analysis is unclear. When the agency does not clearly describe the necessity of the action in the RIA, a third-party reader can not readily evaluate whether or not the proposed alternative addresses the intended need.

Each RIA we reviewed provided an executive summary, including a standardized accounting statement with information on expected benefits and costs in accordance with OMB guidance. Recognizing that executive summaries need to reflect the unique circumstances of each rule, we

---

[13]Market failures occur when the market does not efficiently allocate resources. Circular A-4 states that other compelling public needs may include promoting distributional fairness or privacy.

found that the quality and type of information included in the executive summary was inconsistent across the RIAs. For example, two of the standardized accounting statements—those for CISWI and Boiler MACT—clearly summarized the overall benefits and costs for the selected option and regulatory alternative in the executive summary and compared costs, benefits, and net benefits in a table. Other RIAs, however, did not clearly present this information. For example, EPA listed, but it did not explain the benefits, costs, and other economic effects included in the RFS2 accounting statement. In addition, EPA did not clearly present a net benefits calculation or identify the discount rates used for the estimates. Also, while EPA provided the chapter and section directing readers to more detailed support for the information found in the executive summary, the supporting information was challenging to identify and locate in lengthy chapters, particularly where numbers differed between the executive summaries and the support. In its review of the draft RIA, OMB also raised concerns about the clarity of EPA's presentation of information in the accounting table and provided suggestions for improving its clarity by, for example, adding details in the executive summary explaining each row in the accounting summary statement. When EPA does not present summary-level information in RIAs clearly, accurately, or completely, as called for in OMB guidance, the executive summaries do not provide decision makers and the public with a simple and understandable summary of otherwise lengthy and complex information underlying the rulemaking.

Moreover, for the RIAs we reviewed, EPA did not always provide or clearly present all of the information a reader might need to understand the analysis. OMB guidance states that RIAs should communicate the complex and technical information that supports EPA's regulatory decisions to Congress and the public.[14] Specifically, OMB guidance states that RIAs should enable a third party to understand how the agency arrived at its estimates and conclusions (i.e., clarity and transparency), and Executive Order 12866 states that agencies should provide information to the public in plain, understandable language. However, in the Lead Opt-Out RIA, EPA neither included nor made readily apparent the support for certain benefit estimates in the RIA document, nor did it clearly explain in the RIA the rationale for the regulatory option it chose. Further, in the CISWI RIA, EPA clearly

---

[14]The seven RIAs we reviewed ranged from about 140 to 1,100 pages in length.

presented benefits and costs, but it did not explain the rationale for selecting an alternative that did not yield the greatest net benefits. EPA officials told us they included this information in the preamble of the rule and technical memoranda that were not referenced in the RIA. EPA officials said it was not necessary to include such information in the RIAs because it appeared in these other documents, which are also part of the rulemaking record. However, OMB staff told us they view the RIAs as stand-alone documents that should include relevant information or incorporate references to other documents, so that the support for agency decisions is understandable. Because the RIAs we reviewed did not always provide or clearly present key information, the RIAs' usefulness for providing readers with a clear understanding of the analyses EPA conducted varied.

Senior EPA officials said the RIAs go through several reviews within the agency's ADP, and EPA's National Center for Environmental Economics sometimes participates in reviewing RIAs during their development. Under the federal standards for internal control, federal agencies are to employ control activities, such as management review, to help ensure that management's directives are carried out to achieve effective results.[15] However, the agency's regulatory reviews did not fully ensure the accuracy, transparency, and clarity of information presented in, or among, the RIAs we reviewed. As a result, EPA has not fulfilled its responsibility to provide the public with a clear explanation of the economic information supporting its decision-making process consistent with OMB guidance. We identified additional examples of limited transparency and clarity that specifically relate to other selected elements of the RIAs we reviewed that we describe below.

EPA Generally Adhered to Guidance for Analyzing Regulatory Alternatives, but Its Consideration and Presentation Were Sometimes Limited

For each of the seven RIAs we reviewed, EPA generally adhered to OMB guidance for analyzing regulatory alternatives, but its consideration of alternatives and presentation of the underlying analysis varied. For five of the seven RIAs, EPA analyzed more than one alternative, but, in two of those cases, EPA analyzed only the selected option and one other alternative, while, in the other three cases, it analyzed a broader range of alternatives. OMB guidance recommends that agencies consider and

---

[15]GAO, *Standards for Internal Control in the Federal Government*, GAO/AIMD-00-21.3.1 (Washington, D.C.: November 1999).

present a range of alternatives in an economic analysis, which could involve varying the level of stringency, compliance dates, or requirements for different-sized firms, for example. According to the guidance, considering a range of alternatives can enhance an agency's ability to identify the alternative that yields the greatest net benefits. However, the guidance also states that the number and choice of alternatives selected for detailed analysis is a matter of judgment and, that in making this decision, analysts should consider a balance between thoroughness and practical limits on analytical capacity.

For the two RIAs in which EPA considered the selected option and one other alternative, CISWI and Boiler MACT, EPA considered the two options to which the law specifically refers. Specifically, under the Clean Air Act, EPA sets emission standards based on the maximum achievable control technology or "MACT" in a two-step process. First, EPA identifies the "MACT floor," which is the maximum achievable reduction in emissions of certain air pollutants.[16] Second, EPA selects as its standard either the applicable MACT floor identified in the first stage or a "beyond the floor" limitation more stringent than the MACT if such a standard is achievable in light of costs and other considerations.

In three other RIAs—ELG, Medium- and Heavy-Duty GHG, and Lead Opt-Out—EPA considered a broader range of alternatives. For example, in the Medium- and Heavy-Duty GHG analysis, EPA considered five alternatives along a continuum of stringency, with two alternatives that were less stringent than the selected regulatory alternative and two that were more stringent. EPA concluded in the RIA that the most stringent alternative—the one that would reduce the most emissions—would require advanced technologies that were likely not feasible. Nonetheless, EPA officials said information on this alternative was useful for comparing options in the rulemaking and for informing future decisions.

For the remaining two RIAs—RFS2 and SPCC—EPA presented information for only the selected option. For RFS2, EPA officials said they did not consider analyzing other alternatives because the key purpose of

---

[16]For new sources, the MACT floor is the emission control that is achieved in practice by the best controlled similar source, as determined by EPA; for existing sources, the MACT floor is the average emission limitation achieved by the best performing 12 percent of the existing sources. Natural Resources Defense Council v. E.P.A., 489 F.3d 1250, 1254 (Boiler MACT); 1255-56 (CISWI) (D.C. Cir. 2007).

the RIA was to summarize the impacts of a congressional mandate. Specifically, the Energy Independence and Security Act of 2007 specified the volumes of renewable fuels that must be used in transportation fuel.[17] According to EPA officials, committing agency resources to analyzing additional scenarios was not justifiable given their limited discretion for selecting other regulatory options under the mandate. For SPCC, EPA considered alternatives for several of the amendments in the rulemaking; however, it did not present them in the RIA. EPA officials said the agency presented the alternatives in an RIA that supported an earlier rulemaking, subsequently amended by the SPCC rule we reviewed and, therefore, did not need to include them in the current version.[18] By not including this information, or at least a clear reference to it in the more recent RIA, it was difficult to discern that EPA considered regulatory alternatives and whether the selected approach provided the greatest net benefit.

As discussed above, for certain rules, EPA officials said they had limited discretion in the type of regulatory alternative the agency could implement. Where applicable, OMB guidance directs agencies to consider alternative regulatory approaches that rely on economic incentives (market-based approaches) such as fees, or informational remedies such as product labeling requirements, and offers increased flexibility because these approaches are generally more cost effective than prescriptive approaches. Of the seven RIAs we reviewed, however, only the Medium- and Heavy-Duty GHG RIA considered market-based techniques. For example, under the alternatives analyzed in this RIA, truck manufacturers could earn credits if they adopted certain emission control technologies, providing some incentive to use more advanced technologies.

In addition, several RIAs presented limited information about the regulatory alternatives EPA analyzed. OMB guidance states that agencies should clearly identify alternatives and explain reasons for selecting one alternative over another. Some RIAs did not clearly present this information or presented only limited information. For example, EPA

---

[17]Pub. L. No. 110-140, Title II, 121 Stat. 1519 (2007).

[18]In December 2008, EPA amended the SPCC rule and completed an RIA for that rulemaking. However, the effective rulemaking date was delayed and, upon additional review, was amended by the SPCC rule promulgated on November 13, 2009. The RIA for the new rule built upon the RIA completed for the earlier rulemaking, but it did not include certain key information. Notably, it did not include its analysis of regulatory alternatives.

did not describe the alternatives it analyzed in the Boiler MACT RIA or identify the associated net benefits for each of the alternatives in the Lead Opt-Out RIA. As a result, it was difficult to determine what alternatives the agency considered and whether it selected the alternative that would provide the greatest net benefit. For CISWI, EPA selected an alternative that did not maximize net benefits and did not explain its rationale in the RIA. Instead, EPA officials directed us to a separate technical document that clearly explained the rationale. By not including such an explanation in the RIA, or providing a reference to the technical document containing the rationale, EPA did not fulfill the direction in OMB guidance to provide a transparent pathway for understanding the rationale for its selected regulatory approach.

EPA Varied in Its Adherence to Guidance for Estimating Benefits and Costs

In the RIAs we reviewed, EPA varied in its adherence to OMB's guidance for estimating benefits and costs. EPA did not always adhere to OMB guidance stating that RIAs should clearly describe an economic baseline from which the agency measured incremental economic effects. EPA generally adhered to OMB guidance for providing information on benefits and costs for the regulatory alternatives under consideration and using OMB's recommended discount rates. However, EPA faced challenges in two key areas—monetizing certain benefits and costs and estimating the effects of its regulations on employment—that limited the usefulness of some of the estimates in its RIAs. Finally, in several RIAs, EPA used current guidance to estimate the value of carbon dioxide emission reductions and, at the same time, used OMB's overall guidance for conducting RIAs to estimate other benefits and costs.

EPA Did Not Always Clearly Describe an Economic Baseline from Which Benefits and Costs Were Measured

For four of the seven RIAs we reviewed, EPA clearly described economic baselines from which it measured benefits and costs, but it did not do so for the other three. OMB guidance identifies the need for a clearly stated baseline to properly evaluate the benefits and costs of regulatory alternatives. EPA clearly described and explicitly identified the baselines used for the RFS2, SPCC, Medium- and Heavy-Duty GHG, and ELG RIAs, but it did not do so for the CISWI, Boiler MACT, and Lead Opt-Out RIAs. As a result, we had to speak with EPA officials to understand the baseline the agency used in these analyses. Without clearly presenting baselines in these three RIAs, EPA did not fulfill its obligation to transparently provide information necessary for a third party to evaluate the agency's estimates and conclusions.

According to OMB guidance, baselines should reflect the expected state of the world without the regulation. In developing baselines, OMB guidance directs agencies to consider factors such as the evolution of the market, changes in regulations, and the degree of compliance by regulated entities with other regulations. Each of the RIAs we reviewed developed and used baselines that took one or more of those factors into account; however, one of the RIAs relied on outdated baseline information. Specifically, the RIA for the 2009 SPCC rule used the baseline from a 2002 SPCC rule, despite EPA having revised certain aspects of that rule in 2006. EPA officials said their use of the older baseline was still relevant because the revisions made in 2006 had not yet been fully implemented. By not using a more current baseline, EPA may not have presented the most up-to-date depiction of the expected state of the world from which to compare regulatory alternatives.

EPA Generally Adhered to OMB Guidance on Providing Information on Benefits and Costs of Regulatory Alternatives

In the seven RIAs we reviewed, EPA provided information on the benefits and costs—monetized, quantitative, and qualitative—for all the alternatives considered. According to OMB guidance, agencies should monetize quantitative estimates wherever possible. All seven of the RIAs we reviewed monetized some benefits for the regulatory alternatives considered, including, for example, expected improvements in human health as a result of air pollution reductions. All but one of the RIAs monetized some costs. Specifically, the SPCC RIA did not quantify or monetize the potential costs to the environment associated with reducing the regulatory burden on farms and other entities. The remaining six RIAs estimated both monetized benefits and costs but, for one of these, EPA did not present net benefits—a key outcome of conducting these analyses, according to OMB's guidance.[19] For the Lead Opt-Out RIA, EPA officials said they did not present the net benefits calculation because doing so would have implied more precision and certainty in the benefits estimates than the data warranted. Without a reliable estimate of net benefits for each alternative, however, a third-party reader cannot determine whether the agency selected the alternative that maximized net benefits.

When monetization or quantification is not possible, OMB guidance states that agencies should explain why and present a detailed description of the qualitative effects, as well as a discussion of the strengths and

---

[19]OMB's Circular A-4 states that benefit-cost analysis provides an indication of the most efficient alternative—the one that generates the largest net benefits to society—which is useful information for decision makers and the public even when economic efficiency is not the only or primary consideration.

limitations of that information.[20] Each of the RIAs we reviewed included a qualitative discussion of some potential benefits and costs, and most explained why EPA could not quantify them. However, some RIAs did not present a complete discussion of the strengths and limitations of the qualitative information. For example, the Lead-Opt Out RIA contains more than 10 pages of qualitative information about the health and environmental effects associated with lead exposure, but it does not discuss the strengths and limitations of the information as it pertains to the regulatory action. Without such information, the potential significance of these effects on the overall analysis is unclear.

To determine the present value of monetized benefits and costs agencies expect to occur in future years, OMB guidance states that agencies should apply discount rates of 3 and 7 percent, unless a different rate is justified.[21] EPA generally used OMB's recommended discount rates to estimate benefits and costs in all of the RIAs we reviewed; however, in the RFS2 RIA, EPA did not clearly present its discounted estimates of benefits and costs using both rates, making it difficult to discern whether the agency used a consistent rate in the calculation.[22] In other RIAs, EPA clearly presented such information. For example, in the CISWI RIA, EPA clearly delineated the estimated benefits, costs, and net benefits at the 3 and 7 percent discount rates for both alternatives in two separate tables that were concise and easy to follow.

OMB guidance also states that, when monetizing benefit and cost estimates in RIAs, agencies should generally estimate benefits and costs to society and should include any significant effects of regulations on private entities. In its analysis of the Medium- and Heavy-Duty GHG regulation, EPA estimated that more than 80 percent of the benefits would accrue to private entities—individual truck owners and operators—

---

[20]OMB's Circular A-4 and Regulatory Impact Analysis: A Primer.

[21]OMB Circular A-4 states, for example, that if a rule will have important intergenerational benefits or costs, the agency might consider a further sensitivity analysis using a lower discount rate in addition to calculating net benefits using discount rates of 3 and 7 percent.

[22]For the ELG rule, EPA used undiscounted cost estimates and some undiscounted benefits for their net benefits analysis. According to EPA officials, the use of undiscounted estimates was appropriate because it reflected EPA's estimate of a long-term activity level in the industry, rather than one captured in a relatively near-term projection analysis.

in the form of fuel cost savings.[23] According to the final RIA, including this private benefit in the overall benefit estimate resulted in total benefits that exceeded overall compliance costs, yielding a positive net benefit.

According to OMB guidance, when estimated cost savings exceed estimated compliance costs, the agency should examine and discuss why market forces would not accomplish these gains in the absence of regulation.[24] The RIA discussed conceptually several reasons why truck buyers might not purchase more fuel-efficient vehicles in the absence of the regulation, identifying market failures such as incomplete information or industry-wide barriers that prevent truck buyers from minimizing costs. EPA officials told us that to estimate the value of greater fuel efficiency and all other truck product attributes, they held constant these other attributes, such as size and torque, before and after the regulation. By assuming that these attributes remained constant, EPA officials reasoned that the costs of these attributes would be higher and therefore result in a more conservative estimate of net benefits. However, EPA's assumptions and associated cost adjustments were not readily transparent in the RIA. Moreover, because EPA did not integrate both costs and consumer behavior into one consistent model, EPA may have misstated the value or benefits resulting from increased fuel efficiency. OMB staff said the data needed to account for these offsetting factors often do not exist. Moreover, EPA did not explore nonregulatory alternatives that could correct a market failure, such as providing truck buyers with more information about fuel economy through product labeling or other means as OMB guidance recommends.

EPA Faced Challenges in Two Key Areas That Limited the Usefulness of Some of the Estimates in Its RIAs

In assessing EPA's adherence to OMB guidance, we identified two key areas in which EPA faced challenges that limited the usefulness of some of the estimates in its RIAs—nonmonetized benefits and costs related to the primary purpose or key impacts of the regulatory actions and EPA's approach for estimating the effects of regulations on employment.

---

[23]EPA estimated fuel savings of $34 billion (84 percent of total benefits) at the 7 percent discount rate and $50 billion (87 percent of total benefits) at the 3 percent discount rate.

[24]In other words, the agency should explain why truck owners and operators did not buy higher fuel efficiency vehicles that appear to offer cost savings absent the regulation. In this example, the businesses that purchase and operate medium- and heavy-duty trucks generally operate with narrow profit margins, with fuel costs representing a substantial operating expense. Economic theory suggests that consumers would be willing to pay for increased fuel economy that exceeded the cost of providing it.

In several RIAs, EPA provided quantitative estimates for the benefits and costs related to the primary purpose or key impacts of the regulatory action; however, EPA did not monetize some of these key benefits and costs. OMB guidance acknowledges that monetization is not always possible, and EPA officials said that limited data, modeling capabilities, and time and resource constraints precluded them from monetizing these effects in some cases. For example, in the RIA for RFS2, a rule aimed at increasing the use of renewable fuels such as ethanol and other biofuels through the production of agricultural and other feedstocks, EPA quantified some adverse water quality effects of the renewable fuel standard but did not monetize these effects. EPA officials said they used models to quantify the amounts of nitrogen pollution in water expected from the rule but were not able to use the model to place an economic value on this pollution, citing that limited time and resource constraints precluded them from developing such an economic value. Several water quality experts we spoke with suggested that monetizing water quality effects for this rule may have been possible, but they acknowledged challenges to doing so. For example, experts explained that it is challenging to monetize water quality effects at the national level. In the SPCC RIA, EPA officials said that monetizing potential costs to the environment associated with reducing the regulatory burden on farms and other entities is challenging, in part, due to a lack of information about the likelihood of an oil spill and its effects on the environment.

Further, in the RIAs for two regulations—CISWI and Boiler MACT—aimed at reducing emissions of specific air pollutants, EPA quantified the amount of reductions expected for particular pollutant emissions, but it did not monetize the health benefit associated with those emissions reductions. In the RIAs, EPA explained that methodological and time limitations under court-ordered schedules for the CISWI and Boiler MACT regulations precluded them from monetizing these effects. Specifically, EPA stated in the RIAs that insufficient information existed for emissions from specific sources that prevented the agency from modeling changes in population exposures to ambient concentrations of hazardous air pollutants. Nonetheless, consistent with OMB guidance, EPA included in the RIAs monetized benefits related to reducing particulate matter—a complex mixture of several components, including acids, metals, and soil or dust particles—both as a surrogate for metal hazardous air pollutants and as a secondary benefit resulting from other hazardous air pollutant reductions. Without further research to eliminate data gaps and enhance modeling capabilities to support monetizing additional benefits and costs, however, EPA's RIAs may continue to be limited in their usefulness for understanding economic trade-offs among regulatory alternatives.

In addition, in the RIAs we reviewed, EPA estimated the effects of its regulations on employment in two ways. Executive Order 12866 directs agencies to assess any adverse effects on employment resulting from regulations, but neither it nor OMB's associated guidance provides specific direction on estimating these effects when the outlook is for continued high unemployment. First, in most of the RIAs we reviewed, EPA incorporated certain labor cost estimates in its compliance cost estimates within the benefit cost analyses. To develop these estimates, consistent with Circular A-4, EPA generally assumed the economy was at full employment and, accordingly, that the regulations would displace few workers over the long term, and any individuals laid off as a result of the regulations would quickly find new jobs at comparable wages.

During the time EPA conducted these analyses, however, the United States experienced an economic recession followed by a sluggish recovery with an unemployment rate of 9 percent or higher until late 2011.[25] Some researchers have raised questions about the reasonableness of the full employment assumption, suggesting that the cost of job losses may be substantial and generate other social costs or benefits when the outlook is for continued high unemployment.[26,27] Researchers and senior EPA and OMB officials said that empirically assessing these employment effects is challenging, however, due to data limitations and the inherent difficulty of separating the effects of regulations from other factors in the economy. In addition, some rules have compliance periods that begin and extend well into the future, and EPA officials said that the employment rate during the compliance period is more important than the employment rate when the rule is written. Nonetheless, in the RIA for the Medium- and Heavy-Duty GHG rule, finalized in 2011, EPA qualitatively discussed the possibility that the rule would have a net positive effect on employment by reducing involuntary unemployment.

---

[25]The economic recession began in December 2007 and ended in June 2009, according to the Bureau of Labor Statistics. For comparison, the natural rate of unemployment has ranged from about 5 to 6 percent, according to Congressional Budget Office data.

[26]Richard D. Morgenstern, "Analyzing the Employment Impacts of Regulations," *Does Regulation Kill Jobs?* (Philadelphia, Pennsylvania: University of Pennsylvania, 2013).

[27]Specifically, a regulation that displaces workers during such periods may incur costs if the displaced workers cannot find new jobs at comparable wages. Conversely, a regulation may generate benefits if it reduces involuntary unemployment.

Second, for three of the seven RIAs we reviewed, EPA conducted a separate analysis of the potential effect of its regulations on changes in the number of jobs.[28] Specifically, in the Boiler MACT, CISWI, and ELG RIAs, EPA quantitatively assessed the potential effect of the regulation on employment in the directly affected industries, estimating the expected job losses and gains for each. With limited methods, studies, and models available for assessing the potential effects of regulation on employment, EPA relied primarily on an economic study that had several limitations.[29] For example, the study was based on outdated information that considered the effect of regulations on employment for certain years from 1979 through 1991. In addition, the study was limited to four industrial sectors. By applying this study to its analyses, EPA effectively assumed that the conditions at the time of the study, as well as the sectors considered, were relevant to the conditions and industries affected by the regulations we reviewed. EPA acknowledged in the RIAs that the study has these limitations. In addition, senior agency officials acknowledged the limitations in our discussions and said the authors of the underlying study have since questioned its sufficiency for use in regulatory analyses. However, the officials also said that the study represented the best reasonably obtainable data when they conducted their analyses. EPA officials said they last used the study to support quantitative estimates of employment effects in June 2013, but that the study continues to provide a theoretical framework for EPA's consideration of employment effects in RIAs. In addition, they said they have begun to explore new approaches for analyzing employment effects. However, EPA officials were uncertain about when such information would be available. Without additional information and improvements in its approach for estimating employment effects, EPA's RIAs may be limited in their usefulness for helping decision makers and the public understand the potential effects of the agency's regulations on employment.

---

[28] EPA's analysis of the net change in jobs represents an assessment of the distribution of the benefits and costs among different groups in society, distinct from the analysis of the net social benefits of regulatory alternatives.

[29] Richard D. Morgenstern, William A. Pizer, and Jhih-Shyang Shih, "Jobs Versus the Environment: An Industry-Level Perspective," *Journal of Environmental Economics and Management*, 43 (2002). For the ELG RIA, EPA used the Bureau of Economic Analysis input-output model to estimate employment effects. While the Bureau of Economic Analysis model estimates both positive and negative outcomes for employment in different sectors and is used in many analyses, it also has certain limitations.

EPA Used Current Guidance to Estimate the Value of Carbon Dioxide Emission Reductions

In four of the RIAs we reviewed, EPA estimated the value of carbon dioxide emission reductions using a measure known as the social cost of carbon. A federal interagency working group, co-led by OMB and the Council of Economic Advisers, developed social cost of carbon estimates in a technical support document produced in 2010 and updated in 2013.[30] According to OMB staff, the technical support document guidance—developed by experts from numerous agencies—is an extension of the guidance in Circular A-4, aimed specifically at estimating the value of future reductions of carbon emissions.[31] The 2010 technical support document, which was applicable to most of the rules we reviewed, does not include a clear overall statement of its relationship to Circular A-4, but includes references to Circular A-4 in certain sections of the body that explain how the technical support document guidance relates to the general direction provided in Circular A-4. Similarly, the 2013 update of the technical support document references Circular A-4 in the body, but does not include a clear overall statement of its relationship to Circular A-4.

The benefits and costs of reducing most greenhouse gas emissions, including carbon dioxide, differ from other benefits and costs in at least two respects: (1) greenhouse gas emissions contribute to global damages even when emitted in the United States because these emissions disperse widely throughout the atmosphere and (2) these emissions generally remain in the atmosphere for years, causing subsequent long-term damages. As a result, the technical support document represents an approach for estimating the value of reducing future carbon dioxide emissions that differs from the approach for estimating other benefits and costs described in Circular A-4 in two key ways.

First, while Circular A-4 states that agencies should generally estimate domestic benefits and costs of regulations, it also provides latitude to include global economic effects resulting from regulations when relevant

---

[30]Interagency Working Group on Social Cost of Carbon, *Technical Support Document: Social Cost of Carbon for Regulatory Impact Analysis under Executive Order 12866* (Washington, D.C.: February 2010). OMB and the Council of Economic Advisers are both offices within the Executive Office of the President.

[31]According to the technical support document, the purpose of the social cost of carbon estimates is to allow agencies to incorporate the social benefits of reducing carbon dioxide emissions into benefit-cost analyses of regulatory actions that have marginal impacts on cumulative global emissions.

and states that such effects should be reported separately and in addition to domestic effects. According to the more recent technical support document, a global measure of benefits and costs for greenhouse gas reductions is preferable in light of the global nature of climate change. Accordingly, in the four RIAs, EPA estimated the value of reducing future carbon dioxide emissions using a global value rather than focusing solely on benefits that would accrue to the United States. In addition, the technical support document notes that relatively few region- or country-specific models for estimating a domestic measure of the social cost of carbon exist, and the EPA officials responsible for these analyses reiterated this challenge. The technical support document includes a range of values for adjusting the global social cost of carbon to estimate domestic effects based on one model but states that the values are "approximate, provisional, and highly speculative."[32] OMB staff said the interagency working group will continue assessing whether it can generate a more reliable domestic measure.

Second, for valuing reductions of future carbon dioxide emissions using social cost of carbon estimates, the technical support document adapts and revises the guidance in Circular A-4 related to discount rates. Circular A-4 states that agencies should discount future benefits and costs using rates of 3 and 7 percent but notes that agencies may, in addition, consider a lower discount rate if a rule will have important intergenerational benefits or costs. OMB has stated, however, that a 7 percent discount rate is not appropriate for valuing carbon dioxide emissions because it does not adequately account for the impact of carbon dioxide emissions on future generations.[33] Accordingly, in the RIAs we reviewed that included estimates related to reducing carbon dioxide emissions, EPA generally applied the technical support document's social cost of carbon estimates based on discount rates of 2.5, 3, and 5 percent.[34] According to OMB, these discount rates are

---

[32]The technical support document states that the interagency working group determined that a range of values from 7 to 23 percent should be used to adjust the global social cost of carbon to calculate domestic effects.

[33]The technical support document also states that using discount rates lower than 7 percent is appropriate. Generally, using a higher discount rate gives less weight to future year benefits and gives more weight to near-term benefits.

[34]The technical support document was finalized in the same month and year as the RIA for the RFS2 rule. Therefore, EPA used the government-wide interim values for social cost of carbon that were in place at the time.

consistent with the latitude provided in Circular A-4 and span a plausible range to account for disagreement in the literature on the appropriate rate to use in this context and various uncertainties. Circular A-4 preceded the technical support document and has not been amended and, accordingly, it does not reference the technical support document or explain the relationship between the two documents. Because Circular A-4 generally suggests that agencies use discount rates of 3 and 7 percent and the relationship to the technical support document is not clear, including estimates of benefits at different discount rates can lead to the appearance that EPA did not adhere to the general direction regarding discount rates in Circular A-4.

Moreover, applying Circular A-4 and the technical support document simultaneously can lead to an inconsistency in some of EPA's net benefits analyses. For example, in the Medium- and Heavy-Duty GHG RIA, EPA estimated the value of reducing future carbon dioxide emissions using a 3 percent discount rate, as provided in the technical support document, and incorporated that estimate with the other non-greenhouse gas benefit and cost estimates it discounted using both the 3 percent and 7 percent discount rates suggested in Circular A-4. Incorporating the estimate for carbon dioxide emission reductions at 3 percent with other benefits and costs discounted at 7 percent produces an analytical inconsistency, whereas incorporating the estimate for carbon dioxide emission reductions at 3 percent with other benefits and costs discounted at the same rate does not. In effect, using a lower discount rate to estimate the value of reducing future carbon dioxide emissions than that used to estimate other benefits and costs places greater weight on carbon dioxide emission reductions when calculating the overall net benefits of a rule.

OMB staff said they understand the issues associated with incorporating carbon dioxide reduction estimates discounted at a lower rate with net benefits discounted at the 7 percent rate. However, they said this difference in discount rates is unavoidable due to the intergenerational nature of the benefits associated with reducing carbon dioxide emissions and noted that the technical support document envisions this possibility— that other benefits and costs unrelated to carbon dioxide emissions will be discounted at rates that differ from those used to develop the social cost of carbon estimates.[35] According to OMB staff, discounting and integrating intergenerational benefits in benefit-cost analyses is an active area in the literature, and the interagency working group has committed to periodically updating the technical support document. However, they told us they have not yet determined a better approach for addressing this analytical issue. Without increased clarity regarding the relationship between Circular A-4 and the technical support document and additional guidance on presenting the analytical inconsistencies, questions about the adherence of the agency's analyses to Circular A-4 and challenges related to the public's understanding of the agency's estimates will likely persist.

EPA Generally Adhered to Guidance on Analyzing Uncertainty and Describing Data Quality

EPA generally adhered to OMB guidance on analyzing uncertainties with key assumptions underlying its RIAs although, in some cases, its assessment of uncertainty was limited. OMB guidance states that analyzing and presenting important uncertainties as part of the overall regulatory analysis can inform the public and decision makers about the effects of these uncertainties on the benefits and costs of alternative regulatory actions. For example, a sensitivity analysis can show how benefit and cost estimates may change under different assumptions. OMB guidance also states that agencies should conduct a formal quantitative analysis of the relevant uncertainties about benefits and costs for rules with estimated annual effects of $1 billion or more.[36]

For all of the RIAs we reviewed, EPA assessed the uncertainty of some key assumptions. For three of the four RIAs with estimated annual effects of $1 billion or more, EPA conducted a formal quantitative analysis. However, for these three RIAs, EPA did not conduct such an analysis of all of the relevant uncertainties, as OMB guidance directs. OMB staff acknowledged that time and resources limitations can hinder agencies' ability to conduct such analyses. In some cases, EPA cited data limitations as the reason for not doing so. In the Boiler MACT RIA, for example, EPA used experts' judgments, among other methods, to assess

---

[35]The technical support document states in a footnote that, "it is possible that other benefits or costs of proposed regulations unrelated to carbon dioxide emissions will be discounted at rates that differ from those used to develop the SCC estimates."

[36]OMB guidance describes a formal quantitative analysis as estimating the probability distribution of regulatory benefits and costs.

the variability in one important component of its benefit estimates—the extent to which emissions of certain air pollutants lead to premature mortality. EPA officials said, however, they did not analyze other relevant uncertainties related to other aspects of these pollutants because of data limitations. Also, in this RIA, EPA did not analyze the uncertainties associated with its cost estimates. EPA officials said that, in weighing time and resource constraints against additional uncertainty analyses for cost estimates, they determined additional analysis was not worthwhile because the benefits of the rule far outweighed the costs, and additional analysis under alternative assumptions would not likely change that conclusion. However, by not assessing uncertainty associated with the cost estimates, the RIA implied greater precision than was warranted.

For the other three RIAs we reviewed, EPA had greater flexibility under OMB guidance because the annual effects of the rule totaled less than $1 billion. Specifically, for rules expected to range in annual effects from $100 million to $1 billion, the guidance suggests that agencies consider using techniques ranging in complexity from a sensitivity analysis to more formal uncertainty analysis. While each of these RIAs analyzed some uncertainties, only one of the three RIAs analyzed most of the relevant uncertainties. For example, in one RIA, EPA did not analyze the uncertainties associated with the cost estimates.

In addition, EPA generally described the quality of data, models, and assumptions underlying its analysis or whether the information had undergone peer review. According to OMB guidance, agencies should rely on peer-reviewed literature, where available, to document their use of the best reasonably obtainable scientific, technical, and economic information in RIAs. In many instances, EPA described the quality of the underlying data and models and the use of peer-reviewed data. For example, in the RFS2 RIA, EPA used a new peer-reviewed model to calculate an important piece of the final analysis, which improved the estimates between the proposed and final rules, according to EPA officials.[37] In other instances, however, EPA did not describe the quality of the underlying data and models. Although EPA explained to us that they aim to have their models peer-reviewed, for CISWI and Boiler MACT, EPA used a non-peer reviewed multimarket model to estimate social

[37]For example, according to EPA, the peer review of its life-cycle analysis enabled the agency to improve its use of satellite imagery by using higher resolution data for its final analysis.

costs and benefits because, according to EPA officials, no peer-reviewed model was available. EPA officials said they used this model, nonetheless, because at the time of the analysis it was considered an appropriate approach. Disclosing such information about the underlying model in the RIA would provide readers with its potential limitations and areas for future improvement. Ultimately, the peer review—completed after EPA used the estimates in the analysis—criticized a number of the assumptions and data used in the model, raising questions about the reliability of these estimates. EPA officials said they no longer use the model and that they plan to revise it in response to the peer review.

Conclusions

RIAs are valuable tools for helping agencies assess whether the benefits of an action justify the costs and identify the regulatory alternative that yields the greatest net benefits. In addition, RIAs provide affected entities, government agencies, Congress, and the public with important information about the potential effects of new regulations, which can result in significant benefits and costs. Because the information in RIAs can be complex and technical, it is important that agencies clearly present how they arrived at their estimates and conclusions. OMB guidance provides best practices for conducting regulatory analysis and communicating this information; however, EPA did not always adhere to this guidance. In particular, EPA's regulatory review process does not ensure that the information about selected elements that should appear in the analyses—such as clear descriptions of baselines and alternatives considered—is transparent or clear, within and across its RIAs. Without enhancements to its review process targeted at improving adherence to OMB guidance, EPA cannot ensure that its RIAs provide the public with a clear understanding of its decision making. In addition, executive summaries are a key focal point of these lengthy, complex RIAs. When the executive summaries are not clearly or accurately linked to the detailed analyses, they do not provide decision makers and the public with simple, understandable explanations of the expected economic effects of the regulations.

In addition, EPA faced challenges in two key areas that limited the usefulness of some of the estimates in its RIAs. First, resource and data limitations constrained EPA's ability to monetize certain benefits and costs related to the primary purposes or key impacts of the rules we reviewed, such as the health benefits of reducing hazardous air pollutants and water quality effects. A key aspect of regulatory analysis is monetizing the benefits and costs, but OMB guidance acknowledges this is not always possible. However, when EPA does not monetize key benefits and costs, the RIAs may be limited in their usefulness for helping decision makers and the public understand economic trade-offs among different regulatory alternatives. Second, because EPA relied on an outdated and limited study to estimate the effects of regulations on employment, it may have inaccurately characterized the relationship between those regulations and employment. EPA officials said they have begun to explore new approaches for analyzing employment effects. However, EPA officials were uncertain about when such information would be available. Without additional information and improvements in its approach for estimating employment effects, EPA's RIAs may be limited in their usefulness for helping decision makers and the public understand the potential effects of the agency's regulations on employment.

Finally, in response to increased emphasis on agencies' ability to monetize the effects of regulations on reductions of carbon dioxide emissions—the effects of which are long lasting and global in nature—a federal interagency working group, co-led by OMB and the Council of Economic Advisers, developed a technical support document for estimating these effects to supplement the guidance in OMB's Circular A-4. EPA's use of the technical support document for estimating the value of reducing future carbon dioxide emissions and Circular A-4 for estimating other benefits and costs in its RIAs has raised questions about the agency's adherence to Circular A-4 and has introduced an inconsistency in EPA's analyses. Without increased clarity regarding the relationship between Circular A-4 and the technical support document, and additional guidance on presenting the analytical inconsistencies, questions about the adherence of agencies' analyses to Circular A-4 and challenges related to the public's understanding of their estimates will likely persist.

Recommendations for Executive Action

We are making six recommendations in this report.

To improve future adherence to OMB guidance for conducting RIAs, we recommend that the EPA Administrator take the following two actions:

- enhance the agency's review process for RIAs to ensure the transparency and clarity of information presented for selected elements in and across RIAs; and
- improve the accuracy, transparency, and clarity of the information included in the executive summaries of each RIA.

In addition, to enhance the usefulness of EPA's RIAs, we recommend that the EPA Administrator take the following two actions:

- identify and prioritize for research key categories of benefits and costs that the agency cannot currently monetize that, once monetized, would most enhance the agency's ability to consider economic trade-offs associated with different regulatory alternatives; and
- continue efforts to update and improve the agency's approach to estimating employment effects.

To clarify the relationship between OMB Circular A-4 and an Interagency Working Group's Technical Support document for estimating the effects of changes in carbon dioxide emissions, and the approach agencies should use when informing decision makers and the public of their findings, we recommend that the Director of OMB consider taking the following two actions:

- clarify the relationship between OMB Circular A-4 and the Technical Support Document by increasing the visibility of relevant language in the Technical Support Document; and
- continue monitoring the economic literature and working with agencies to identify approaches for presenting social cost of carbon estimates with other analytical results that have been discounted at different rates to help agencies more transparently communicate about the circumstances unique to assessing the long-term effects of changes in carbon dioxide emissions.

Agency Comments and Our Evaluation

We provided a draft of this report to EPA and OMB for review and comment. In written comments, which are reproduced in appendix III, EPA generally agreed with our recommendations and described actions it intends to take to address them. Additionally, EPA provided comments on areas in the report where it believes that our findings and conclusions are incomplete or would benefit from a clearer and more robust consideration of context as well as technical comments, which we incorporated as appropriate. In oral comments on behalf of OMB, OMB staff commented on both recommendations and suggested several changes and clarifications, which we used to modify the recommendations. We discussed these changes and clarifications with OMB staff, who said they neither agreed nor disagreed with the revised recommendations but saw some merit in them. OMB staff also commented on technical issues, which we addressed as appropriate.

Regarding the first two recommendations to the EPA Administrator, in its comment letter, although the agency agrees with our recommendations, EPA stated that our findings do not point to systemic deficiencies with respect to the accuracy of the agency's analytic work. EPA also stated that it supports our emphasis on the importance of transparency and clarity and will continue to strive to enhance these qualities in its RIAs. EPA then described actions it plans to take to address these recommendations. In its comments on our findings concerning RIAs, EPA characterized the seven rules we reviewed as a very small subset of RIAs for the rules that EPA has issued in recent years. We disagree with this characterization. The seven rules we reviewed represent more than one-third of the 20 economically significant rules EPA finalized from 2009 through 2011, the period from which we sampled rules. In addition, four of the rules had economic effects of over $1 billion, a threshold beyond which OMB guidance directs agencies to conduct additional analysis because of the significance of these effects. EPA correctly stated that our findings cannot be generalized, which we acknowledged in our report.

Also in its comments on our findings concerning RIAs, EPA stated that the report suggests that the agency's use of the discount rates in the interagency support document for the social cost of carbon raised questions about the agency's adherence to OMB Circular A-4 and about the consistency of analysis in certain RIAs. We believe that our report includes a robust discussion of this issue and related context. Specifically, our report describes the fact that EPA relied on two different guidance documents—OMB Circular A-4 and a Technical Support Document that was developed by OMB and the White House Council of Economic Advisers—for estimating certain benefits and costs. In this context, we identified a challenge related to the clarity of the relationship between these two documents that can lead to confusion about whether EPA adhered to OMB Circular A-4—the primary guidance document that agencies should use when conducting economic analysis. We therefore recommended that OMB enhance the clarity of the relationship between the two documents.

Regarding the third recommendation to the EPA Administrator, in its comment letter, EPA stated that the agency agreed with the importance of making continual improvements in valuing the benefits and costs of its regulatory actions and is constantly working to improve in these areas. The agency also stated that it will continue to invest in areas that will support improvements in its ability to quantify important benefits and costs, including areas we identified such as water quality benefits and hazardous chemical impacts. In its comments on our related findings concerning the monetization of benefits and costs, EPA accurately characterized the flexibility agencies have to design analyses in ways that optimize the use of limited resources while providing appropriate information about policy options. Furthermore, our report acknowledges this flexibility and identifies challenges EPA faces in monetizing certain types of benefits. In some cases, however, EPA was not able to monetize benefits and costs related to the primary purpose or key impacts of the regulatory action. In these cases, our report points out that this can limit the usefulness of RIAs in helping decision makers and the public understand the potential effects of EPA rules.

Regarding the fourth recommendation to the EPA Administrator, in its comment letter, EPA stated that while the agency considers its current practices to be up-to-date and consistent with sound science and economics, it continues to explore the relevant theoretical and empirical literature and to seek public comments on analysis of economically significant regulations to ensure that the way it characterizes the employment effects of its regulations is valid and informative. In its comments on our findings concerning the agency's analysis of employment impacts, EPA stated that it was important for us to recognize that the agency relied on the best available peer-reviewed research that existed at the time that EPA conducted its RIAs and that the agency's treatment transparently recognized the limitations of the study where it was applied. Although EPA discussed the potential limitations associated with using the study in RIAs we reviewed, the RIAs did not analyze whether factors such as the time period and the industries reflected in the employment study were appropriate for use in these RIAs. In addition, the lead author of the employment study has since indicated that the study should not be used to estimate employment effects in regulatory analyses.

Regarding the first recommendation to the OMB Director, our draft report recommended that OMB draw an explicit link between Circular A-4—the primary guidance document for conducting economic analysis issued in 2003—and later guidance issued in 2010 and updated in 2013 on estimating the effects of changes in carbon dioxide emissions because it was difficult to determine whether EPA's use of the later guidance adhered to Circular A-4. In their oral comments, OMB staff said that an explicit link already exists in the 2010 guidance. We agree that the 2010 guidance had some language explaining the relationship between it and Circular A-4 but that this language did not feature prominently in the 2010 guidance or appear in Circular A-4. As a result, the relationship between the two sets of guidance was still unclear. In response to the OMB comments, we modified the recommendation to say that the Director of

OMB should consider clarifying the relationship between the two sets of guidance to assist the public and decision makers in understanding the results of analyses that follow both guidance documents.

Regarding the second recommendation to the OMB Director, our draft report recommended that OMB provide further guidance on how agencies should present estimates of the benefits of regulations when agencies discount different types of benefits (including changes in carbon dioxide emissions) at different rates because this can introduce inconsistencies in the analytical results that make it difficult for the public and decision makers to understand. OMB staff said that the existing economic literature was unresolved on addressing this issue and that issuing further guidance would thus be premature. In response to the OMB comments, we modified the recommendation to say that the Director of OMB should continue monitoring the economic literature and working with agencies on approaches for presenting estimates of changes in carbon dioxide emissions along with other types of economic effects that have been discounted at different rates.

As agreed with your offices, unless you publicly announce the contents of this report earlier, we plan no further distribution until 30 days from the report date. At that time, we will send copies of this report to the Administrator of EPA, the Director of OMB, the appropriate congressional committees, and other interested parties. In addition, the report will be available at no charge on the GAO website at http://www.gao.gov.

If you or your staff members have any questions about this report, please contact me at (202) 512-3841 or gomezj@gao.gov. Contact points for our Offices of Congressional Relations and Public Affairs may be found on the last page of this report. GAO staff who made key contributions to this report are listed in appendix IV.

J. Alfredo Gómez
Director, Natural Resources and Environment

Appendix I: Objectives, Scope, and Methodology

This report examines how the Environmental Protection Agency (EPA) has used economic analyses in its decision making during the rulemaking process and the extent to which EPA adhered to Office of Management and Budget (OMB) guidance in conducting selected elements of the economic analyses the agency used to support recent rulemakings.

To identify the economic analyses for our review, we used OMB's historical lists of rules it has reviewed to compile a list of the economically significant rules—those with an annual effect on the economy of $100 million or more or that have a material adverse effect on a sector of the economy; productivity; competition; jobs; the environment; public health or safety; or state, local, or tribal governments or communities— EPA finalized in 2009 through 2011. This yielded a total of 20 rules from which we eliminated from consideration four rules: (1) a rule related to National Ambient Air Quality Standards because EPA is statutorily prohibited from considering costs in setting these standards; (2) a rule that EPA identified as erroneously appearing on OMB's list of economically significant rules; and (3) two rules because they applied to specific states, rather than the nation. This reduced our universe of possible rules for consideration to 16 rules. From these, we selected a nonprobability sample of seven EPA rules that met the following criteria: (1) they were considered economically significant under Executive Order 12866; (2) they were finalized from 2009 through 2011; (3) they were conducted by four different EPA program offices (Air and Radiation, Chemical Safety and Pollution Prevention, Solid Waste and Emergency Response, and Water); and (4) they were expected to have a varying range of effects on the economy. Because this was a nonprobability sample, findings from our review of the seven rules cannot be generalized to those we did not review.

To examine how EPA used economic analyses in its decision making, we interviewed EPA officials that prepared the Regulatory Impact Analyses (RIA) and other documentation for each rule, as well as officials from EPA's Office of Policy. They provided detailed explanations about the regulatory decision-making process for each rule and how RIAs were used in that process. In addition, we reviewed the final RIAs for the seven selected rules. To assess the extent to which EPA adhered to OMB's guidance in Circular A-4 for selected elements of the RIAs, we developed a checklist that included questions related to each element and applied the checklist to all seven rules. For each RIA, two analysts (including one economist) independently reviewed the analyses and subsequently came to consensus about each element's adherence to OMB guidance. For each rule, we also reviewed the relevant Federal Register notices

prepared during the course of the rulemaking, draft RIAs, and other
relevant technical documents. We compiled the individual checklists into
a summary checklist to assess the extent to which the rules as a group
adhered with specific elements of OMB Circular A-4 principles. The
selected elements we examined included: the analyses' overall
transparency and use of executive summaries and statements of need;
treatment of regulatory alternatives; estimation of benefits and costs; and
treatment of uncertainty, assumptions, and descriptions of data quality.

To enhance our understanding of the analyses, we interviewed the EPA
officials that prepared the RIAs from the four EPA offices, including the
Offices of Air and Radiation, Chemical Safety and Pollution Prevention,
Solid Waste and Emergency Response, and Water. In addition, to
increase our understanding about specific categories of estimates, we
reviewed economic literature and interviewed a convenience sample of
economists, selected because of their knowledge and expertise regarding
specific technical issues that appeared in the seven RIAs. Finally, we
interviewed OMB staff to discuss specific elements of OMB Circular A-4
and technical guidance related to estimating the economic effects of
reducing greenhouse gases.

We conducted this performance audit from February 2012 to July 2014 in
accordance with generally accepted government auditing standards.
Those standards require that we plan and perform the audit to obtain
sufficient, appropriate evidence to provide a reasonable basis for our
findings and conclusions based on our audit objectives. We believe that
the evidence obtained provides a reasonable basis for our findings and
conclusions based on our audit objectives.

Appendix II: Rule Descriptions

This appendix includes a brief description of the seven rules we reviewed.

Greenhouse Gas Emissions Standards and Fuel Efficiency Standards for Medium- and Heavy-Duty Engines and Vehicles (Medium- and Heavy-Duty GHG)

On September 15, 2011, the Environmental Protection Agency (EPA) and the Department of Transportation's National Highway Traffic Safety Administration (NHTSA) finalized regulations in a joint rulemaking to establish a comprehensive Heavy-Duty National Program. The respective rules responded to a May 21, 2010, presidential directive and constituted the first-ever program to reduce greenhouse gas emissions and fuel consumption in the heavy-duty highway vehicle sector. In this rulemaking, EPA finalized carbon dioxide emissions standards, and NHTSA concurrently finalized fuel consumption standards for three regulatory categories of heavy-duty vehicles: combination tractors; heavy-duty pickup trucks and vans; and vocational vehicles. EPA set additional standards in its rule, including final hydrofluorocarbon standards to control leakage from air-conditioning systems, and final nitrous oxide and methane emissions standards for combination tractors and heavy-duty pickup trucks and vans. In this rule, EPA also finalized provisions allowing light-duty vehicle manufacturers to use carbon dioxide credits to meet the light-duty vehicle nitrous oxide and methane standards, technical amendments to the fuel economy provisions for light-duty vehicles, and a technical amendment to the criteria pollutant emissions requirements for certain switch locomotives. EPA's final greenhouse gas emission standards under the Clean Air Act begins with model year 2014 and will be fully phased in by 2018. This phase of the Heavy-Duty National Program did not regulate commercial trailers.

The agencies estimated that the combined standards will reduce carbon dioxide emissions by approximately 270 million metric tons and save 530 million barrels of oil over the life of vehicles sold during the 2014 through 2018 model years and yield $49 billion in net benefits at a 3 percent discount rate and $33 billion in net benefits at a 7 percent discount rate.

National Emissions Standards for Hazardous Air Pollutants for Major Sources: Industrial, Commercial, and Institutional Boilers and Process Heaters (Boiler MACT)

On March 21, 2011, EPA finalized this rule, which requires industrial, commercial, and institutional boilers and process heaters located at major sources to meet hazardous air pollutants standards reflecting the application of the maximum achievable control technology (MACT).[1] Under section 112(d) of the Clean Air Act, EPA must set these emissions limits for both existing and new sources. For existing sources, the MACT standards must be at least as stringent as the average emissions limitation achieved by the best performing 12 percent of existing sources for which there is emissions information. For new sources, the MACT standards must be at least as stringent as the control level achieved in practice by the best controlled similar source. In both scenarios, these levels are referred to as the MACT floor. EPA also must consider more stringent "beyond-the-floor" control options and, in doing so, must take into account the maximum degree of reduction in emissions of hazardous air pollutants, costs, energy, and nonair environmental impacts. The final rule regulated the following hazardous air pollutants: hydrogen chloride (as a surrogate for acid gases); particulate matter (as a surrogate for nonmercury hazardous air pollutant metals); carbon monoxide (as a surrogate for nondioxin and furan organic hazardous air pollutants); mercury; and dioxin and furan emissions.

EPA estimated the net benefits of this rule to range from $20.5 to $52.5 billion at a 3 percent discount rate and from $18.5 to $47.5 billion at a 7 percent discount rate. The monetized benefits reflect the health benefits associated with reducing exposure to fine particulate matter through directly emitted particulate matter and precursors (such as sulfur dioxide), as well as reducing ozone exposure through reductions of volatile organic compounds. In addition to the monetized benefits, EPA estimated that the rule would reduce 112,000 tons of carbon monoxide; 30,000 tons of hydrogen chloride; 820 tons of hydrogen fluoride; 2,800 pounds of mercury; 2,700 tons of other metals; and 23 grams of dioxins and furans.

---

[1]Section 112(d) of the Clean Air Act requires EPA to set emissions standards for hazardous air pollutants emitted by major stationary sources based on the performance of the maximum achievable control technology.

Regulation of Fuels and Fuel Additives: Changes to Renewable Fuel Standard Program (RFS2)

On March 26, 2010, EPA issued a final rule implementing changes to the National Renewable Fuel Standard program as required under the Clean Air Act Section 211(o), as amended by the Energy Independence and Security Act of 2007 (EISA).[2] The 2007 act expanded the renewable fuel standard established by the Energy Policy Act (EPAct) of 2005.[3] The renewable fuel standard is the mandated minimum volume of biofuels used in the national transportation fuel (gasoline and diesel) supply each year. EISA mandated the use of 36 billion gallons of renewable fuel by 2022, a significant increase over the requirement in EPAct 2005. EISA also required that an increased amount of the mandate be met with advanced biofuels—certain biofuels produced from feedstocks other than corn starch—compared with conventional corn-based ethanol. Specifically, 21 billion of the 36 billion gallon mandate of renewable fuel is expected to come from advanced biofuels by 2022. EPA expects the revised RFS2 to lay the foundation for achieving significant reductions of greenhouse gas emissions from the use of renewable fuels, reducing imported petroleum, and encouraging the development and expansion of our nation's renewable fuels sector.

EPA estimated net benefits of the mandated volumes ranging from $13 to $26 billion. The measure does not include the costs of investments needed to increase renewable fuel production. The agency estimated those capital costs to total $90.5 billion through 2022.

---

[2]Pub. L. No. 110-140, Title II, 121 Stat. 1519 (2007).

[3]Pub. L. No. 109-58, sec. 1501, 119 Stat. 1067 (2005).

Standards of Performance for New Stationary Sources and Emission Guidelines for Existing Sources: Commercial and Industrial Solid Waste Incineration Units (CISWI)

On March 21, 2011, EPA finalized a rule to implement section 129 of the Clean Air Act, which required EPA to develop and adopt standards for new and existing commercial and industrial solid waste incineration units (CISWI), including emissions limitations for nine specific pollutants—particulate matter (total and fine), opacity (as appropriate), sulfur dioxide, hydrogen chloride, nitrogen oxides, carbon monoxide, lead, cadmium, mercury, and dioxins and dibenzofurans.[4] Enacted in 1990, Section 129 required EPA to issue standards for solid waste incinerators that were more stringent than those EPA had proposed in 1989.[5] Under section 129, EPA must set emissions limits based on MACT for both new and existing sources.[6] The rule also requires CISWI units to demonstrate compliance through testing and monitoring.[7]

Five of the nine pollutants subject to section 129 are also regulated as hazardous air pollutants under section 112(c)(6) of the act. During the development of the CISWI rule, EPA was under a court order to issue regulations under section 112(c)(6) by January 16, 2011. Because some CISWI units, including those burning solid waste for energy recovery, are also subject to section 112(c)(6), EPA determined that the CISWI rule was subject to this court-ordered deadline.

In the 2011 rule, EPA expected few new CISWI units to be constructed over the subsequent 5-year time frame, and that those few would be constructed to replace existing units. Standards for both new and existing units are generally more stringent than those previously in effect.

EPA estimated the net benefits of this rule to range from $60 to $550 million at a 3 percent discount rate, and from $30 to $470 million at a 7 percent discount rate.

---

[4]42 U.S.C. § 7429.

[5]Davis County v. EPA, 101 F.3d 1395, 1407 (D.C. Cir. 1996).

[6]The degree of reduction in emissions that is deemed achievable for new units in a category shall not be less stringent than the emissions control that is achieved in practice by the best controlled similar unit, as determined by the Administrator. Emissions standards for existing units in a category may be less stringent than standards for new units in the same category but shall not be less stringent than the average emissions limitation achieved by the best performing 12 percent of units in the category.

[7]The rule also includes a 5-year technology review of the new source performance standards and emission guidelines required under section 129 of the Clean Air Act.

Lead; Amendment to the Opt-out and Recordkeeping Provisions in the Renovation, Repair, and Painting Program (Lead Opt-Out)

In 2008, EPA issued a rule regulating renovation and remodeling activities that create health hazards arising from lead paint (RRP rule). Among the provisions in the rule was an "opt-out" provision, which exempted owner-occupied housing from the rule's requirements if the homeowner certified that no pregnant women or young children lived there. In addition, the RRP rule established certain training, certification, accreditation, and recordkeeping requirements. EPA noted in the 2008 final rule that most commenters did not agree with the opt-out provision as EPA had proposed, but the agency retained the provision in the final rule, though in a somewhat narrower form than originally proposed.[8] Shortly after the rule was published, several petitions challenged the rule, including several from environmental and children's health advocacy groups. On August 24, 2009, EPA signed an agreement with these groups in settlement of their petitions. In this agreement, EPA committed to propose several changes to the RRP rule, including proposing to remove the opt-out provision.

In May 2010, EPA finalized an amendment to the RRP rule removing the opt-out provision, concluding that it is important to require RRP work practices and training and certification requirements in target housing even if there is no child under age 6 or pregnant woman residing there. EPA further supported the amendment stating that implementing the regulations without the opt-out provision promotes, to a greater extent, the Toxic Substances Control Act directive to promulgate regulations covering renovation activities in target housing.

Following the removal of the opt-out provision, trade associations petitioned a federal appellate court for review of the rule.[9] One petitioner, the National Association of Home Builders, argued that EPA's removal of the opt-out amendment was unauthorized because the "only event of note between the inclusion and removal of the opt-out provision was a settlement agreement which obligated the Agency to undertake certain actions." In rejecting this argument and upholding the 2010 rule, the court held that there were two other events which preceded the settlement that explained why EPA reconsidered the opt-out provision: a new President

---

[8]The 2008 final rule excluded housing where pregnant women reside from the opt-out provision.

[9]National Association of Homebuilders v. EPA, 682 F.3d 1032 (D.C. Cir. 2012).

and a new EPA Administrator.[10] The court similarly rejected the contention that EPA's change in position was invalid because EPA had merely revisited old evidence and arguments, rather than relying on new data or experience.[11]

EPA estimated that the rule would cost between $246 and $295 million at a 3 percent discount rate and between $267 and $320 million 7 percent discount rate and yield benefits ranging from $866 million to $3.1 billion at a 3 percent discount rate and from $920 million to $3.3 billion at a 7 percent discount rate.

Oil Pollution Prevention; Spill Prevention, Control, and Countermeasure Rule—Amendments (SPCC)

Under the Clean Water Act, EPA must issue requirements establishing procedures, methods, and equipment to prevent discharges of oil from facilities to navigable waters. The Spill Prevention, Control, and Countermeasure (SPCC) Rule, first promulgated in 1973, outlined actions regulated facilities must take to prevent, prepare for, and respond to oil spills before they reach navigable waters or adjoining shorelines. The rule required each owner or operator of a regulated facility to prepare or amend and implement a plan that describes how the facility is designed, operated, and maintained to prevent the discharge of oil into navigable waters or adjoining shorelines. The plan must include measures to control, contain, clean up, and alleviate the effects of an oil spill to prevent such spills from reaching any navigable waters or adjoining shorelines. Facilities may incur significant costs to develop, revise, and implement an SPCC plan. The costs depend on, among other things, the size and type of facility and whether the facility is new or existing.

In December 2008, EPA amended the SPCC rule to, among other things, exempt several types of facilities from some or all of the rule's

---

[10]683 F.3d at 1043. The court relied on a statement by Justice Rehnquist in a previous case: "A change in administration brought about by the people casting their votes is a perfectly reasonable basis for an executive agency's reappraisal of the costs and benefits of its programs and regulations. As long as the agency remains within the bounds established by Congress, it is entitled to assess administrative records and evaluate priorities in light of the philosophy of the administration." Motor Vehicle Mfrs. Ass'n of U.S., Inc. v. State Farm Mut. Auto. Ins. Co., 463 U.S. 29, 59 (1983) (Rehnquist, J., concurring in part and dissenting in part).

[11]683 F.3d at 1037. The court relied on the majority opinion in State Farm, which held that "an agency's view of what is in the public interest may change, either with or without a change in circumstances." 463 U.S. at 57 (internal punctuation and citations omitted).

requirements. The effective rulemaking date, however was delayed and upon additional review was amended.[12] On November 13, 2009, EPA promulgated a new rule that amended the December 2008 SPCC amendments to, among other things, make technical corrections and remove three provisions it had previously finalized as exemptions. Specifically, upon additional review, and after consideration of additional public comments, EPA removed the exclusion of farms and oil production facilities from the loading/unloading rack requirements because EPA did not believe there was a basis to treat these facilities differently from other facilities with loading/unloading racks. In addition, EPA removed two other exemptions—the exemption for produced water containers and the alternative qualified facility eligibility criteria, both applicable to oil production facilities—because EPA determined that these measures would not effectively protect the environment from oil discharges. EPA stated that removal of these provisions would increase compliance costs but reduce the risk of oil spills.

Overall, EPA estimated total cost savings for the final amendments of $95 million at a 7 percent discount rate. The agency did not present a net benefit calculation as it did not monetize the costs associated with the rule.

---

[12]In January 2009, the incoming administration directed agencies to consider extending by 60 days the effective date of rules, such as the SPCC rule, that had been published in the *Federal Register* but that had not yet taken effect. OMB provided guidance to the agencies listing several factors that might justify this 60-day extension, including "whether the rule reflected proper consideration of all the relevant facts." For this reason, EPA delayed the effective date of the SPCC rule until April 2009, and it requested additional comment on the rule. In April, EPA further delayed the effective date of the rule until January 2010, so it could continue considering the comments it had received. EPA issued the revised SPCC rule in November 2009.

GAO-14-519 EPA's Economic Analyses

Effluent Limitations Guidelines and Standards for the Construction and Development Point Source Category (ELG)

On December 1, 2009, EPA finalized regulations establishing Clean Water Act technology-based effluent limitations guidelines (ELG) and new source performance standards for storm water discharges from the construction and development industry. The regulations require that discharges from construction sites disturbing 10 or more acres of land at one time meet a numeric turbidity limit, among other things. In addition, all construction sites that are currently required to obtain a National Pollutant Discharge Elimination System permit must limit erosion and control sediment discharges from construction sites. The final rule became effective on February 1, 2010. In January 2011, EPA stayed implementation of the numeric limit.[13] The other portions of the rule remain in effect.

EPA planned to phase in the numeric ELG over 4 years. Beginning 18 months after the effective date of the final rule, construction sites that disturb 20 or more acres at one time would have been required to monitor site discharges and comply with the numeric effluent limitation. Beginning 4 years after the effective date of the final rule, construction sites that disturb 10 or more acres at one time would have been required to monitor site discharges and comply with the numeric effluent limitation.

EPA estimated that compliance with the ELG and new source performance standards would reduce the amount of sediment and other pollutants discharged from construction and development sites by approximately 4 billion pounds per year. The agency also estimated that compliance with this regulation would provide approximately $369 million in annual monetized societal benefits and $959 million in annual societal costs, which would result in a negative net benefit (or net cost) of $590 million at a 3 percent discount rate.

[13]Following the issuance of the 2009 rule, three trade associations filed petitions for review in federal court. In addition, in April 2010, the Small Business Administration filed with EPA a petition for administrative reconsideration of several technical aspects of the 2009 rule, including potential deficiencies with the dataset that EPA used to support its decision to adopt the numeric turbidity limit. In response to these petitions, EPA agreed to reconsider this limit. In December 2012, EPA settled the court cases by agreeing to issue a proposed rule that would, among other things, withdraw the numeric turbidity limit. EPA issued this proposed rule in April 2013.

Appendix III: Comments from the U.S. Environmental Protection Agency

UNITED STATES ENVIRONMENTAL PROTECTION AGENCY
WASHINGTON, D.C. 20460

JUL - 9 2014

OFFICE OF
POLICY

Mr. Alfredo Gomez
Acting Director
Natural Resources and Environment
U.S. Government Accountability Office
441 G Street, N.W.
Washington, DC 20548

Dear Mr. Gomez:

Thank you for the opportunity to review and comment on the U.S. Government Accountability Office's draft report, "EPA Should Improve Adherence to Guidance for Selected Elements of Regulatory Impact Analyses" (GAO-14-519). The purpose of this letter is to provide the Environmental Protection Agency's response to your recommendations. Although the EPA generally agrees with GAO's recommendations and is committed to continual improvement in the clarity of its regulatory impact analyses, the Agency does not believe that the handful of issues identified by GAO indicate any systematic deficiencies with respect to the accuracy of our analytical work. Further, we wish to highlight a number of areas in which we believe the report's findings and conclusions are incomplete or would benefit from a clearer and more robust consideration of context.

Consistent with E.O. 12866, the EPA develops RIAs for all of its economically significant regulations. The RIAs are reviewed by the Office of Management and Budget, undergo an interagency review, and are then released for public notice and comment along with the proposed rulemaking before being revised for the final rule. The Agency relies on the best available information to calculate both the costs and benefits of our rules, and uses the public comment process to further refine that work. Other economists have observed that "RIAs conducted by the EPA consistently rank at or near the top of the 17 agencies considered for all three categories of openness, analysis, and use."[1] That said, the Agency constantly strives to improve both the quality and transparency of its RIAs and looks forward to building upon GAO's feedback to further improve its work.

In its examination of a very small subset (seven) of RIAs for the rules which the EPA has issued in recent years, GAO found that the EPA generally adhered to OMB Circular A-4. Because this was such a small sample, GAO itself acknowledges that the results "cannot be generalized" to the EPA's economic analyses overall. Nevertheless, GAO identifies several areas, particularly RIA executive summaries, where in GAO's view the EPA could have been clearer, could have achieved greater consistency among RIAs, or where information made available in other parts of the rulemaking package could have been more clearly reflected in the RIA.

---

[1] R. Morgenstern, see http://www.rff.org/RFF/Documents/RFF-DP-11-17.pdf

As a general matter, the EPA believes it is important to understand and acknowledge the real-world context in which RIAs are conducted. OMB Circular A-4 itself acknowledges that RIAs must balance "thoroughness and practical limits of analytical capacity." OMB Circular A-4 thus contemplates that agencies must have some flexibility to design analyses in ways that optimize use of limited resources while providing appropriate information about policy options. The EPA may also choose not to monetize an effect if to do so would require significant additional analytical resources but the relevant effect would likely be negligible relative to the other benefits categories that were monetized. In addition, scientific and economic methods do not yet provide all the answers needed to monetize all costs and benefits even in the face of unlimited resources.

Further, the EPA believes that certain of GAO's findings and conclusions are incomplete or would benefit from a more robust explanation of context. First, GAO's report suggests that the Agency's use of the discount rates in the interagency technical support document for the social cost of carbon raised questions about the Agency's adherence to OMB Circular A-4 and about the consistency of analysis in certain RIAs. As GAO notes, however, OMB and the Council of Economic Advisers convened an interagency group to develop the technical support document in order to extend the guidance in OMB Circular A-4 by developing a way for agencies to incorporate the social benefits of reducing greenhouse gases into the benefit-cost analysis of regulatory actions. Further, as GAO also acknowledges, OMB has explained that it regards the discount rates in the social cost of carbon technical support document as consistent with OMB Circular A-4 and the available economic literature.

Second, GAO's report concludes that failure to monetize some benefits in certain RIAs makes it more difficult for the public to fully understand economic trade-offs. The EPA agrees that there are challenges in completely monetizing both benefits and costs; in particular, the EPA is often unable to quantify or monetize all of the public health and environmental benefits of its regulations, including some potentially important effects. However, the report does not fully acknowledge that this is a broad problem in benefit-cost analysis which is not unique to the EPA, nor that the EPA puts significant effort into clearly indicating benefit categories for which the Agency is unable to monetize benefits. Further, when it is not possible to monetize all impacts, qualitative analysis of non-monetized impacts provides the best available information to communicate to the public.

Third, the EPA believes it important to clarify certain points raised by GAO with regard to the Agency's analysis of employment impacts. In recent years, the EPA has significantly increased the amount of employment analysis in its RIAs. The EPA does not use the same approach for employment analysis for every rule. As with other analyses in our RIAs, each employment analysis is tailored to the specifics of that regulation and reflects the degree to which reliable tools and data are available to quantify impacts. Employment analysis poses broadly recognized analytical challenges, and when conducting such analysis the EPA consistently uses the best tools and data available for the relevant rulemaking. In some cases, the EPA focuses on a qualitative discussion of the employment impacts – both positive and negative – and in other cases, it quantifies selected employment impacts. As the GAO acknowledges, the Agency strives in all instances to transparently describe the strengths and weaknesses of the approach chosen by the Agency. The EPA believes that these analyses, whether qualitative or quantitative, provide decision-makers and the public with the most reliable information available on the employment impacts of its rules and has worked hard to refine these analyses over time.

GAO's discussion of employment impact analysis focuses on one particular study that the EPA used to quantify employment effects in two of the seven rules reviewed by the GAO. It is important to recognize that this study represented the best available peer-reviewed research at the time these RIA's were conducted and the EPA's treatment transparently recognized the limitations of the study where it was applied. The EPA recognizes that there are limited tools provided in the peer-reviewed economics literature to quantify the small shifts in employment that might be attributable to environmental regulation. As discussed below, the EPA is already engaged with the academic community to seek better tools in this area.

GAO Recommendations

Moving forward, the EPA will work to respond to GAO's recommendations:

- **Enhance the agency's review process for RIAs to ensure the transparency and clarity of information presented for selected elements in and across RIAs; and**
- **Improve the accuracy, transparency, and clarity of the information included in the executive summaries of each RIA.**

EPA Response: The EPA stands behind the quality of RIAs that we conduct and believes the GAO findings do not point to systematic deficiencies with respect to the accuracy of our analytical work. That said, the Agency supports GAO's emphasis on the importance of transparency and clarity and will continue to strive to enhance these qualities in our RIAs. The EPA's Office of Policy, and particularly the National Center for Environmental Economics, will continue to work within the Agency's existing Action Development Process to promote transparency and clarity in RIAs. The EPA's *Guidelines for Preparing Economic Analyses* (December 2010) describe principles for presenting the results of economic analyses, with a particular emphasis on a thorough and transparent presentation of benefits and costs. This includes effective presentation of effects that cannot be quantified and/or put into dollar terms. The Office of Policy will issue a memo to program offices reaffirming the importance of transparency and clarity in RIAs, particularly the executive summary, and will work to incorporate greater emphasis of these points in the economic analysis component of the Agency's Action Development Training conducted at the Agency twice a year.

- **Identify and prioritize for research key categories of benefits and costs that the agency currently cannot monetize that, once monetized, would most enhance the agency's ability to consider economic trade-offs associated with different regulatory alternatives; and**

EPA Response: The Agency agrees with the importance of making continual improvements in valuing the benefits and costs of our regulatory actions and is constantly working to improve in these areas. The social cost of carbon represents an excellent example of a benefit that was unquantified prior to 2008, but is now included in the EPA's RIAs. The EPA is currently working in other important areas of economic valuation as well. For example, the EPA is in a long term process of examining the factors that affect the estimated costs of regulations in a retrospective study of the costs of the EPA regulations. This could help to identify systematic differences between ex post and ex ante compliance cost estimation and, ultimately, allow for improvements in the way in which cost analyses are done. The Agency is also in the process of seeking input from an independent expert Science Advisory Board panel on modeling economywide impacts. The EPA will continue to invest in areas that will support improvements in our ability to quantify important benefits and costs, including areas identified by GAO such as water quality benefits and hazardous chemical impacts.

- **Continue efforts to update and improve the agency's approach to estimating employment effects.**

<u>EPA Response:</u> While the EPA considers our current practices to be up-to-date and consistent with sound science and economics, the EPA continues to explore the relevant theoretical and empirical literature and to seek public comments on analysis of economically-significant regulations in order to ensure that the way the Agency characterizes the employment effects of its regulations is valid and informative. In October of 2012, the Agency convened a scientific workshop with academic experts to examine the theory and methods for understanding employment effects of environmental regulation. The Agency is in the process of updating its *Guidelines for Preparing Economic Analyses* to include a revised employment impacts section. Recent RIAs, including the proposed Residential Wood Heaters New Source Performance Standard in January 2014 and the final Tier 3 Vehicle Emission and Fuel Standards Program in March 2014, have used some of the updated literature review, description of theoretic models, and empirical methods for employment impact analyses that will be incorporated into the update to the *Guidelines*. Finally, the Science Advisory Board panel examining modeling economy wide impacts will include discussion of approaches to capture employment effects.

Thank you again for the opportunity to review the draft report. If you have questions or need further information, please contact Jennifer Bowen (202-566-2281).

Sincerely,

Joel Beauvais
Associate Administrator

cc: Janet McCabe
James Jones
Mathy Stanislaus
Nancy Stoner
Laura Vaught
Al McGartland
Bob Trent

4

Appendix IV: GAO Contact and Staff Acknowledgments

GAO Contact	J. Alfredo Gomez, (202) 512-3841, or gomezj@gao.gov
Staff Acknowledgments	In addition to the individual named above, Michael Hix, Assistant Director; Ulana Bihun; Barbara El Osta; Cindy Gilbert; Tim Guinane; Richard P. Johnson; Jamie Meuwissen; Susan Offutt; and Alison O'Neill made key contributions to this report. Armetha Liles and Justin Mausel also contributed to this report.

GAO's Mission	The Government Accountability Office, the audit, evaluation, and investigative arm of Congress, exists to support Congress in meeting its constitutional responsibilities and to help improve the performance and accountability of the federal government for the American people. GAO examines the use of public funds; evaluates federal programs and policies; and provides analyses, recommendations, and other assistance to help Congress make informed oversight, policy, and funding decisions. GAO's commitment to good government is reflected in its core values of accountability, integrity, and reliability.
Obtaining Copies of GAO Reports and Testimony	The fastest and easiest way to obtain copies of GAO documents at no cost is through GAO's website (http://www.gao.gov). Each weekday afternoon, GAO posts on its website newly released reports, testimony, and correspondence. To have GAO e-mail you a list of newly posted products, go to http://www.gao.gov and select "E-mail Updates."
Order by Phone	The price of each GAO publication reflects GAO's actual cost of production and distribution and depends on the number of pages in the publication and whether the publication is printed in color or black and white. Pricing and ordering information is posted on GAO's website, http://www.gao.gov/ordering.htm. Place orders by calling (202) 512-6000, toll free (866) 801-7077, or TDD (202) 512-2537. Orders may be paid for using American Express, Discover Card, MasterCard, Visa, check, or money order. Call for additional information.
Connect with GAO	Connect with GAO on Facebook, Flickr, Twitter, and YouTube. Subscribe to our RSS Feeds or E-mail Updates. Listen to our Podcasts. Visit GAO on the web at www.gao.gov.
To Report Fraud, Waste, and Abuse in Federal Programs	Contact: Website: http://www.gao.gov/fraudnet/fraudnet.htm E-mail: fraudnet@gao.gov Automated answering system: (800) 424-5454 or (202) 512-7470
Congressional Relations	Katherine Siggerud, Managing Director, siggerudk@gao.gov, (202) 512-4400, U.S. Government Accountability Office, 441 G Street NW, Room 7125, Washington, DC 20548
Public Affairs	Chuck Young, Managing Director, youngc1@gao.gov, (202) 512-4800 U.S. Government Accountability Office, 441 G Street NW, Room 7149 Washington, DC 20548

Please Print on Recycled Paper.